Extra Help for ESL Writers

Supplement to Accompany
Diana Hacker's

A Writer's Reference
Sixth Edition

Marcy Carbajal Van Horn
Santa Fe Community College

BEDFORD / ST. MARTIN'S   Boston ◆ New York

Manufactured in the United States of America.

2   1   0   9   8   7
f   e   d   c   b   a

For information, write: Bedford/St. Martin's, 75 Arlington Street, Boston, MA 02116   (617-399-4000)

ISBN-10: 0–312–45233–0
ISBN-13: 978–0–312–45233–9

Acknowledgments

Averil Coxhead, excerpt from sublist 1 of "A New Academic Word List" published in *TESOL Quarterly* 34. Copyright 2000. Reprinted with permission.
Robert MacNeil and William Cran, excerpt from *Do You Speak American?* Copyright 2005 by Neely Productions, Inc., and William Cran. Reprinted with permission.

H

Extra Help for ESL Writers

H Extra Help for ESL Writers

No matter what your educational background is, entering a college environment will most likely provide opportunities for new ways of doing things. Even if you speak English fluently, it is possible to find college intimidating at first. Sections H1–H4 focus on ways to make your transition to college smooth and successful.

H1

Understanding college-level expectations

In the United States, college classrooms are interactive—students are expected to participate in discussions and sometimes work together in groups. Students are also treated as adults who are responsible for managing their own course work and schedule. Succeeding in this environment may require you to adjust your habits both inside and outside the classroom.

H1-a Read your syllabus carefully.

At the beginning of the semester, your instructor will give you a syllabus, a document that provides critical information about the course, including assignments, grading policies, and your instructor's contact information. (For a sample syllabus, see p. H-4.) Be sure to read through your syllabus carefully so that you will know your instructor's expectations and refer to it often during the term. College students are usually expected to keep up with the course work outlined in a syllabus without reminders from their instructor.

When you look at the syllabi for all your courses, you may find that you have several major assignments due on the same day. You may also have smaller assignments that overlap. A calendar or a schedule maker can help you keep track of the due dates for all your classes. It is a good idea to check your syllabus or your calendar regularly, especially before each class session, to remind yourself of the readings and other assignments.

H1-b Understand the expectations of American classrooms.

Education is a cultural activity, and classroom emphases and expectations vary across the globe. Some cultures value memorization of traditional texts, while others value creative thinking. Some

SAMPLE SYLLABUS

ENG 1101: College Composition I

Instructor: Dr. Morgan Felix

Phone: (321) 234-5678

❶ **E-mail address:** mfelix@yourcollege.edu

Office: Anderson Hall, room 312-B

Office hours: Monday, Wednesday, and Friday, 1:00-2:30 p.m., or by appointment

Course Description

College Composition I (ENG 1101) is designed to give you training and practice in developing literacy in academic English. In this course, you will read and analyze academic texts, and you will write about those texts with an analytical purpose. Multiple drafts are expected for each writing assignment.

Course Objectives

1. Students will learn that writing is a process that requires planning, drafting, revising, peer reviewing, and editing.
2. Students will be competent in reading and analyzing college-level texts.
3. Students will be competent in structuring essays appropriate for college courses, using standard English conventions.

❷ **Required Textbooks**

Kennedy, X. J., Dorothy M. Kennedy, and Jane E. Aaron. *The Bedford Reader*. 9th ed. Boston: Bedford, 2006.

Hacker, Diana. *A Writer's Reference*. 6th ed. Boston: Bedford, 2007.

Grading System

Your final grade will be based on the following:

- Take-home essays, including drafts = 60%
- In-class (timed) essays = 20%
❸ - Attendance and participation = 10%
- Final exam = 10%

Schedule of Readings and Assignments

You are required to complete the assigned readings *before* each class. Major assignments are listed in **bold**.

❹   BR = Reading assignments from *The Bedford Reader*
    AWR = Reading assignments from *A Writer's Reference*

SAMPLE SYLLABUS (continued)

Week	Day	Class topics	Readings/ assignments due	
1	Tu	Introduction to the course/syllabus		
	Th	In-class diagnostic essay		
2	Tu	Writing description essays	*BR*: pages 135-58 *AWR*: C1 and C2	**5**
	Th	Essay 1 workshop (focus on global revisions)	Essay 1, draft 1 due *AWR*: C3-a and C3-b	
3	Tu	Essay 1 workshop (focus on editing)	Essay 1, draft 2 due *AWR:* C3-c	
	Th	Strategies for taking essay tests	**Essay 1 final draft due**	**6**

1 Instructors want to talk to their students. Often they list contact information and office hours on the course syllabus.

2 A syllabus often includes a list of materials to purchase.

3 Most instructors expect students to participate in class. Participation is often part of the final grade.

4 Abbreviations used in the schedule are explained.

5 Readings for each class are listed in the right-hand column.

6 Major deadlines are listed in bold.

emphasize individual learning; others expect students to work together.

In the United States, college courses typically require creative, original thinking rather than rote memorization. Most courses expect students to work together at least some of the time. Students might learn their course material in the following ways:

- by participating in class discussions
- by learning the rules, patterns, and theories and then applying them to a variety of situations
- by synthesizing (connecting) ideas from multiple sources
- by working with others to develop new approaches or hypotheses

While you might sometimes be required to memorize or learn basic facts and principles, your instructors will most often expect you to move beyond memorization and show original thinking about the content of the course. The following examples are questions from exams in introductory economics classes. The first example is from a class that emphasized memorization of facts; the second is from a class where students were expected to apply concepts to everyday situations.

EMPHASIS ON MEMORIZATION

QUESTION	What does "opportunity cost" mean?
ANSWER	"Opportunity cost" is the value of a resource measured in terms of the next-best alternative use of that resource.

EMPHASIS ON ORIGINAL THINKING

QUESTION/TASK	Illustrate the concept of "opportunity cost" with an example from your own life.
ANSWER	The opportunity cost of going to the movies with my roommate last night was the extra time I could otherwise have spent studying for my economics exam. In other words, I gave up extra study time by going to the movies.

To answer the second question, students needed to learn the definition of *opportunity cost*. But they were expected to go beyond the definition and do some creative thinking.

H1-c Participate actively in class and in groups.

Because US colleges value creativity and originality, students (especially in smaller classes or sections) are expected to participate in class — to share their ideas about the course material, to work together in groups, and sometimes even to lead class discussions. Because students' contributions are so highly valued, many instructors devote a portion of the final course grade to "class participation."

Class participation

To increase your chances of success, take an active part in class discussions. Remember that your instructors will not always expect you to merely recall or restate an idea from the text or a previous class. More often, they will ask you to show original thinking (see H1-b). If you sit quietly, your instructor might assume that you don't know the material or that you have come to class unprepared.

If you feel intimidated by class discussions, you can often overcome your fears by preparing well beforehand. Actively read all of the assigned materials before class and try to anticipate some of the discussion topics your teacher might offer. (Many instructors list the class topics for each session in the course syllabus.) Explore your thoughts and reactions to possible topics before class by keeping a reading journal or by freewriting after you have finished a portion of the assigned reading. Review your written notes a few minutes before class so that you can share your ideas when discussion begins in class.

Working in groups

Group work, or collaborative activity, gives students the chance to learn not only about the assigned course work but also about how to accomplish a task with a variety of team members. An assignment for an environmental studies course, for example, might require you to learn about the levels of toxins in the local water supply for the past five years. If the assignment is a group project, it can help build communication and leadership skills. The group members will need to determine what tasks are required to complete the assignment, and then they will need to divide those tasks among themselves. They might have to choose leaders to coordinate their efforts. Group work also results in a broader understanding of an issue. The group's final report on the water supply will include contributions from all group members, much more information than a person working alone could gather.

Collaborative work might be difficult to adjust to if you come from a culture that emphasizes individual learning or if your high school teachers did not assign group projects. But be prepared to encounter group work in college: Most instructors feel that it creates an atmosphere in which new ideas can emerge. It also serves as preparation for the professional world, where many jobs require some form of collaborative activity.

Showing respect for your peers

While instructors may encourage you to give your own interpretations of material, to argue a point using information in the textbook, or to apply original thinking to basic concepts, remember that most instructors expect you to respect your peers' ideas. In some cultures where certain types of aggression or exhibitions of authority are valued, it may be appropriate to challenge individuals directly by saying that they are wrong or by exposing their personal flaws. In the United States, however, directly challenging a classmate in this manner is considered rude and inappropriate. If you disagree with someone's opinion, it is often best to state that you disagree with the idea—not with the person who said it—and then to explain your reasons with evidence or examples. Likewise, you should state your own opinions and interpretations in a reasonable tone and expect that other students will want to discuss your ideas or even to politely disagree.

Speaking in English

The ability to speak two or more languages is an asset that you should take pride in, but it is also important to be sensitive to your instructor and classmates in your shared learning environment. Whenever possible, use the language that all participants in the class can understand easily. In US academic settings, this language is English. If you feel the need to discuss or explain an idea in your native language with one of your classmates, be sure to alert your instructor first. If you begin speaking to a friend in a language your instructor does not understand, your instructor may think that you are not paying attention (which is considered rude). Try to think of the class time as a regular opportunity to practice your spoken English.

H1-d   Attend classes regularly; arrive a few minutes before each class begins.

Attending class regularly is important for success. Attending class not only will reinforce the material that you have studied on your own but also will provide you with additional opportunities for language practice. You'll have to listen to your instructor and classmates and participate in the discussion. You'll also have to practice reading what your instructor writes on the board (or displays on a screen) and practice writing by taking notes. The classroom experience provides valuable repetition of key ideas and important facts that you will most likely have to recall or apply on tests and assignments.

Your instructors will expect you to arrive at each class a few minutes before the period begins so the discussion can start at the scheduled time. Make a habit of arriving about five minutes before class begins, and use the time to scan your textbook or review your notes from the previous class or from your reading. It is usually much easier to follow the class discussion—especially if your listening skills are not yet fluent—when you review the material first.

H1-e Get extra help when necessary.

If you have questions about the course material or problems with an assignment, do not be afraid to seek extra help. You may get the answers you need from individuals at your school, or you may find useful advice on the Internet.

Writing centers

Most colleges have writing centers (sometimes called *writing labs*) staffed with instructors or experienced students, usually called *writing tutors*. They can assist you at various stages of the writing process. The tutors are typically trained to help in the following areas:

- generating ideas for a writing assignment
- suggesting ways to revise a draft
- identifying areas of a draft that need clarification
- pointing out places in a draft where more development is needed
- diagnosing repetitive mistakes in a paper

It is important to remember that writing center tutors provide guidance, not proofreading services. They are there to help you to grow as a writer—to understand assignments, to learn how to analyze your own writing. They are not there just to "fix" your mistakes. The more prepared you are for your visit and the more willing you are to discuss your problems, the more productive your time with the tutor will be.

Before you visit the writing center, think about specific problems you are having with your assignment. Maybe you don't know what the assignment is asking you to do. Maybe you have a lot of sources but you don't know how to organize them. Maybe you're stuck on one paragraph. Make a list of specific problems and try to organize them into several questions you can ask the tutor. Bring materials related to your assignment to show the tutor as useful background: the assignment itself, an outline if you've done one, notes, drafts, and source materials. Be prepared to discuss your problems actively—to ask the tutor questions and to respond to questions the tutor asks you.

Professor's office hours

In some cultures, visiting a professor's office may be considered disrespectful. However, professors in American colleges usually encourage students to visit them during their office hours. Check your course syllabus to determine when your instructor is available. If you are confused by an assignment or uncertain about any course material, don't be afraid to ask your instructor for help.

Helpful Web sites

Many online writing centers and ESL Web sites provide helpful information and exercises for practice. Here are a few of them.

- *Activities for ESL Students*
  <http://a4esl.org>
  This site, sponsored by the *Internet TESL Journal*, provides quizzes, tests, exercises, and puzzles submitted by ESL teachers.

- *Guide to Grammar and Writing*
  <http://grammar.ccc.commnet.edu/grammar>
  This site includes comprehensive coverage of everything from punctuation to research, using clear examples and detailed explanations. It also includes quizzes on various grammar and writing issues.

- *Randall's ESL Cyber Listening Lab*
  <http://esl-lab.com>
  This site has a wide variety of exercises—from the everyday to the academic—which provide audio files for listening and quizzes to assess comprehension.

- *Ultralingua Online Dictionary*
  <http://ultralingua.com/shared/references/english/index.htm>
  This site is a glossary of grammatical terms. It includes a brief definition and several examples for each term.

- *Voice of America: Wordmaster*
  <http://voanews.com/specialenglish/wordmaster/index.cfm>
  This news and information site allows users to read along as they listen to audio files of articles about English grammar and usage. The site also includes word games and quizzes.

H2

Strategies for improving your academic English

Few residents of the United States speak academic English in all situations every day. Most of us regularly speak an informal variety: We speak in sentence fragments, we use slang, and we use regional forms. However, we must use academic English when we want to reach broader audiences—particularly in college or business settings.

As you aim to improve your performance in academic English, you might need to broaden the range of strategies you use. You might try a number of reading or listening activities, for example, or make an effort to do more grammar exercises. You may decide to consult a dictionary or a thesaurus more regularly or to keep a vocabulary notebook. Such strategies provide practice that can help you gain familiarity with academic English.

H2-a Engage in intensive and extensive language activities.

Languages—including academic English—are learned through both intensive and extensive practice. Intensive practice involves focusing on a small amount of material with a very high level of attention. Completing grammar exercises, for instance, is an intensive activity. A grammar exercise will help you develop control over a very specific grammatical concept, such as past-tense verbs or the use of commas.

Extensive practice involves absorbing a larger quantity of information, typically over a longer period of time. Extensive practices focus less on individual words or forms and more on general comprehension and fluency—your ability to understand, use, and think in English without translating from your native language. Listening to the radio for general understanding is an extensive practice that can help you develop your speed and your grasp of "natural" English forms in various contexts.

The chart on page H-12 gives some everyday examples of intensive and extensive language activities. (Section H4-b provides a list of writing prompts that can be used for both intensive and extensive practice.)

H2-b Read while listening.

If you learned English informally (through conversation rather than in a classroom) or if your middle school and high school classes did not cover English grammar thoroughly, you may need to pay special attention to the differences between spoken English and academic written English. Writing English requires different skills from those used when speaking English. You need to train your *ears* to know what sounds natural, but you also have to train your *eyes* to know what standard English forms look like.

Sample activities for intensive and extensive language practice

	INTENSIVE	EXTENSIVE
READING	■ reading a textbook chapter for content ■ reading difficult material with unfamiliar vocabulary ■ reading essays to understand different organizational styles or grammatical patterns	■ reading novels or nonfiction books for pleasure ■ reading newspapers or magazines regularly ■ reading Web sites or blogs for entertainment
WRITING	■ writing an essay for class or for a test ■ writing a formal letter, application, or résumé ■ completing grammar exercises that focus on specific grammatical concepts	■ e-mailing friends, chatting online, blogging ■ keeping a journal or diary regularly ■ freewriting or fiction writing for enjoyment
LISTENING	■ listening to take notes or to follow directions (in class) ■ listening to dictation to record text accurately ■ listening for specific words, sounds, or intonations	■ listening to friends talk ■ listening to TV shows or movies to get a general idea ■ listening to the radio
SPEAKING	■ giving a formal speech ■ practicing careful pronunciation ■ emphasizing or focusing on specific grammatical forms (such as the past tense) while speaking	■ having a conversation with English-speaking friends ■ chatting on the phone ■ participating in class discussions

If you speak English well but are having trouble using standard forms or correct English spelling when you write, try reading and listening at the same time. Most libraries carry books on CD or tape, and some libraries even package the paper and audio books together. If you read a book while you listen to the audio version of the book, your brain will begin to connect the visual forms with words you've already heard before. If you purchase a paper copy of the book, you can also underline or highlight new words—or words that look different from how they sound—while you listen. After finishing a few pages or a chapter, stop the tape or CD and review the new forms you've marked. Combined reading and listening practice can help you understand standard English forms and use them in your own writing.

The following Web sites provide text and audio—you can listen to someone speak the words as you read along.

- *American Stories on VOA Special English*
  <http://voanews.com/specialenglish/amer-stories-page.cfm>
  Listen to and read short stories by American authors.

- *VOA Special English News Radio for English Learners*
  <http://voanews.com/specialenglish>
  Listen to current global news (broadcast by the US government) while reading the text.

- *The Poets.org Listening Booth*
  <http://poets.org/audio.php>
  Hear famous poets read their own works as you read along.

- *Global English Salon*
  <http://globalenglishsalon.com>
  Listen to and read short editorials and conversations that focus on business English.

H2-c Use an English-English dictionary or a thesaurus.

Many students who learn English in their home country before coming to the United States use bilingual dictionaries, which list words in English with native-language translations or vice versa. By now, you have probably noticed that some words in these dictionaries do not have appropriate translations for academic work. While the dictionaries can help you understand as you read and may help beginning writers, they are not always the best resource for college writing.

Since you are now a college-level writer, consider investing in an English-English dictionary that is designed for multilingual writers. These dictionaries typically provide not only definitions but also sample sentences for each word. Many of these dictionaries also provide information that is not readily available in dictionaries for native speakers. For example, they usually note whether a noun is count, noncount, or both, and they often provide information about the word's level of formality. The following are some dictionaries and thesauri (books that provide lists of synonyms, words with similar meanings) designed for multilingual writers.

DICTIONARIES

- *Cambridge Advanced Learner's Dictionary*
- *Collin's COBUILD Advanced Learner's English Dictionary*
- *Longman Advanced Dictionary of American English*
- *Oxford ESL Dictionary for Students of American English*
- *Random House Webster's Dictionary of American English: ESL/Learner's Edition*

THESAURI

- *Longman's Language Activator*
- *Webster's New Explorer Thesaurus*

H2-d Become familiar with the Academic Word List.

Linguists (researchers who study language and word usage) have identified the most frequently used words in academic texts from all disciplines and have compiled them in a list that they call the Academic Word List. Since you will encounter these words regularly both in textbooks and in class, it's a good idea to familiarize yourself with them early in your college experience if you don't know them already. The chart on page H-15 presents the sixty most commonly used academic words.

H2-e Learn how prefixes and suffixes affect a word's meaning.

A prefix is added to the beginning of a word to expand or change the word's core meaning (its *root* or *stem*). The prefix *non-*, for instance, added to the root word *toxic* changes the meaning of the word from "poisonous" to "not poisonous." The chart on page H-16

Academic Word List

analyze	define	indicate	proceed
approach	derive	individual	process
area	distribute	interpret	require
assess	economy	involve	research
assume	environment	issue	respond
authority	establish	labor	role
available	estimate	legal	section
benefit	evident	legislate	sector
concept	export	major	significant
consist	factor	method	similar
constitute	finance	occur	source
context	formula	percent	specific
contract	function	period	structure
create	identify	policy	theory
data	income	principle	vary

Source: Averil Coxhead, "A New Academic Word List," *TESOL Quarterly* 34 (2000): 213–38, app. A, sublist 1.

will help you become familiar with some common prefixes, their meanings, and some words in which you might encounter them.

Suffixes are word endings that indicate a word's part of speech (noun, verb, adjective, adverb, and so on). Some languages, such as Chinese and southeastern Asian languages, use word order rather than suffixes to convey a word's grammatical function; pay particular attention to suffixes if your language is one of them.

Consider the English noun *democracy*, for example, which has many related forms: *democrat* (a noun), *democratize* (a verb), *democratic* (an adjective), and *democratically* (an adverb). If you were to switch any of these two words in a sentence, your readers might become confused:

       democracy.
We live in a ~~democratic.~~
    ^

The chart on page H-17 will help make you more aware of how a word's suffix determines its part of speech. For descriptions of the parts of speech, see B1 in *A Writer's Reference*.

Prefixes and their meanings

PREFIX	BASIC MEANING	EXAMPLES
a-, an-	without, not	apolitical (not political); anaerobic (without oxygen)
ante-	before	antecedent (an element that comes before something); antebellum (before war, particularly the US Civil War)
anti-	against	antibiotic (medicine that works against bacteria); antiwar (against war)
auto-	self	autobiography (biography of oneself); automatic (self-acting)
bi-	two	biannual (occurring every two years); bicultural (being part of two cultures)
co-, col-, com-, con-, cor-	together, with	coincide (happen together); collaborate (work with); commiserate (be unhappy together); congregate (assemble together); correspond (communicate with)
dis-	opposite, not	disagree (not agree); disappear (opposite of appear)
ex-	out, former	exclude (keep out); ex-president (former president)
il-, im-, in-, ir-	not	illegal (not legal); impatient (not patient); incompatible (not compatible); irresponsible (not responsible)
inter-	between	international (between countries)
intra-, intro-	within, inward	intracultural (within one culture); introspective (reflecting, looking within oneself)
intro-	in, into	introduce (bring in)
mis-	wrong, bad	mislead (lead someone in the wrong direction); misuse (use wrongly)
mono-	single, only	monopoly (control by one person or group); monotheism (belief in one God)
non-	not, without	nonverbal (without speech); nontraditional (not traditional)
omni-	all	omniscient (all-knowing); omnivorous (eating all foods)
pan-	all	panacea (cure for all diseases); pantheon (temple of all gods)
poly-	many	polygamy (marriage to more than one person at one time); polyglot (a person who speaks many languages)
post-	after, later	postmodern (after the modern period); postpone (put off till later)
pre-	before	prejudice (judgment before sufficient knowledge); prepare (make something ready)

PREFIX	BASIC MEANING	EXAMPLES
pro-	forward	proceed (go forward); progress (move forward)
re-	again	reappear (appear again); redo (do again)
sub-	under	submarine (underwater vessel); subway (underground train)
super-	over, more than, huge	superimpose (place something over another); superpower (huge power)
un-	opposite, not	unimportant (not important)

Suffixes and their parts of speech

NOUNS

-acy	aristocracy, democracy, privacy, supremacy
-ance, -ence	assistance, dependence, independence, science
-ancy, -ency	emergency, delinquency, infancy, vacancy
-dom	boredom, freedom, kingdom, wisdom
-er, -or	computer, stapler, writer, counselor
-hood	brotherhood, childhood, motherhood, neighborhood
-ism	Buddhism, communism, journalism, perfectionism
-ist	chemist, dermatologist, pianist, socialist
-ity, -ety, -ty	liberty, unity, society, variety
-ment	enjoyment, environment, government, replacement
-ness	forgetfulness, goodness, happiness, sadness
-ship	courtship, friendship, membership, partnership
-sion, -tion, -ion	admission, immigration, pollution, vacation

VERBS

-ate	anticipate, complicate, cooperate, reiterate
-ify	amplify, mystify, quantify, terrify
-ize	computerize, demonize, maximize, publicize

ADJECTIVES

-able, -ible	drinkable, edible, forgivable, legible
-al	functional, legal, physical, visual
-ent, -ient	obedient, salient, sentient, silent
-ful	beautiful, hopeful, powerful, regretful
-ic	automatic, egocentric, poetic, systematic
-ive	active, extensive, passive, productive
-less	fruitless, harmless, homeless, useless
-ous, -ious	delicious, delirious, gracious, mysterious

ADVERBS

-ly	easily, convincingly, hopefully, quickly

H2-f Keep a vocabulary notebook.

Use a vocabulary notebook to keep track of new words—especially those that you have seen more than one time or that you have seen in a few different places. You can make a vocabulary notebook in a binder with loose-leaf paper (single sheets), in a bound journal, or in a simple composition book. While you are reading for your classes, jot down a few new words in your notebook, along with the sentences in which you found the words. After you finish reading, look up each word in an English-English dictionary (see H2-c). Record the word's definition and part of speech, and scan the dictionary page for related words. If you look up the noun *effect*, for instance, you will find in the same entry or on the same page the verb *effect*, the related adjective *effective*, the noun *effectiveness*, and the adverb *effectively*. Keeping track of related words is an easy way to expand your vocabulary with little effort. See the sample vocabulary notebook entry below.

ON THE WEB > dianahacker.com/writersref
    ESL help > Blank vocabulary notebook pages

H2-g Keep an editing log.

As part of the writing process, you will be reading and rereading your own writing to make sure your ideas are clearly stated and to correct any grammatical errors you may have made. Your editing

SAMPLE VOCABULARY NOTEBOOK ENTRY

Word: *civilized*   **Form: Noun Verb (Adj.) Adv.**
                        Other _____

Meaning: **Related words:**
Sophisticated, developed   *civil (adj.)*
                        civilize (v., transitive)
                        civilian (n., person)
                        civilization (n.)

Sentence: *The Romans believed that the Germanic tribes from the north were not civilized.*

SAMPLE EDITING LOG 1: CHECKLIST

Editing log (1/07-5/07)

Issues	Paper 1	Paper 2	Paper 3	Paper 4	Paper 5
Subject-verb agreement	✓✓✓✓	✓✓✓	✓	✓	
Verb tense	Past ✓✓✓ Future✓✓	Past ✓✓			Past ✓
Verb form	Be + -ing form ✓✓✓	Be + -ing form ✓			
Passive voice	✓✓	✓✓	✓	✓	✓
Comma splice	✓✓✓✓	✓✓			
Fragment	✓				
Missing article	✓✓✓✓✓✓	✓✓✓✓✓	✓✓✓✓	✓✓✓	✓✓
Wrong article	✓✓✓✓	✓✓	✓✓	✓	
Missing plural form	✓✓✓✓✓	✓✓✓	✓✓✓	✓✓	✓

SAMPLE EDITING LOG 2: CORRECTED SENTENCES

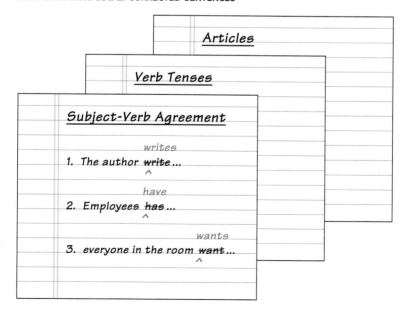

Articles

Verb Tenses

Subject-Verb Agreement

       writes
1. The author ~~write~~ ...
       ^

       have
2. Employees ~~has~~ ...
       ^

       wants
3. everyone in the room ~~want~~ ...
       ^

process can be more effective if you keep an editing log or notebook of common errors you make or areas of grammar that give you particular trouble.

When you get a paper back from an instructor, record in your notebook any errors your instructor marked. You might also record any grammatical points that you looked up as you were writing or editing. Your log might be a single chart or checklist, as in sample 1 on page H-19. Or it might consist of sentences with errors and the corrections you make to them, as in sample 2.

Each time you write a new paper, check your editing log during the final stage of your writing process to help you track down and correct your typical mistakes.

H2-h   Target specific areas for improvement.

As you master academic English, you will draw on four main skills—reading, writing, speaking, and listening—and you will develop those skills at different rates. At this point, for example, you may have more control over spoken English than formal grammar, or you may have stronger reading skills than listening skills. To increase your chances of success in college, strive to balance out your skills so that you can rely on strengths in not just one or two but all four skill areas.

It may help to work with an instructor or adviser to create a plan that identifies areas for improvement and lists strategies that will help you build your skills.

ON THE WEB > dianahacker.com/writersref
ESL help > Strategies for improving your academic English

H3

Academic writing and cultural expectations

As you challenge yourself to grow as an academic writer, pay particular attention to your readers' expectations. Some researchers have called English a "writer-responsible" language: The writer (particularly in academic and business settings) is responsible for taking a stand on an issue, stating a clear thesis, and making his or her ideas obvious to readers. Many other languages are "reader-responsible": Writers show many sides to an issue but leave the interpretation entirely to readers.

If you are accustomed to a "reader-responsible" culture, you might find English writing too direct and assertive. Keep in mind, however, that academic readers in the United States will expect you to make a clear point and to convince them with evidence and examples that your ideas are valuable and worthy of their consideration.

H3-a In most academic papers, assert your claim before providing the evidence.

Readers in most academic situations will expect to see your claim— your thesis or main idea—before seeing your evidence or support for the claim (see C2-a and A2-e in *A Writer's Reference*). This is quite different from academic styles in some other languages, which leave the main point open to readers' interpretations or which conclude the essay with the main idea rather than begin with it.

If you're not accustomed to stating a thesis before providing support, you might find it useful to outline your essays carefully before beginning to write. (See also C1-d in *A Writer's Reference* for details on outlining.) Consider using the following steps until you feel comfortable with the academic English style:

1. Outline your ideas in the method with which you are familiar (for example, with the main idea or claim at the end).
2. Read your outline and highlight the main idea and the supporting points in your outline.
3. Rearrange your outline so that the main idea is at the beginning.
4. Use your rearranged outline as a guide when you draft your essay.

Don't be concerned if this planning stage takes time. Remember that the planning stage of writing often takes longer than the writing stage does.

The first sample outline on page H-22 shows several points of support, leading up to the main point in the last sentence. The revised outline shows the preferred organization for an academic English essay, with the main point stated first, followed by the evidence or support.

ORIGINAL: MAIN IDEA LAST

1. In the United States, teenagers often move out of their parents' homes when they turn eighteen.

2. The parents' money is considered only the parents' money--not the money of their adult children.

3. Without their parents' financial help, young American adults often scramble to find affordable housing, transportation, and jobs to pay for all their needs.

4. The fast pace of their daily activities and their lack of job security can be very stressful.

5. So while independence is typically an attractive feature of American culture, it is not always positive.

REVISED: MAIN IDEA FIRST

1. While independence can be an attractive feature of American culture, it can put negative pressure on young people.

2. In the United States, teenagers move out of their parents' homes when they turn eighteen.

3. The parents' money is considered only the parents' money--not the money of their adult children.

4. Without their parents' financial help, young American adults often scramble to find affordable housing, transportation, and jobs to pay for all their needs.

5. The fast pace of their daily activities and their lack of job security can be very stressful.

NOTE: In most cases, paragraphs also should state the main point first, followed by supporting evidence (see C4-a in *A Writer's Reference*). There are, however, some exceptions to this pattern, particularly in the introductory and concluding paragraphs of an essay (see C2-a and C2-c).

H3-b Take a stand on an issue.

As an academic writer, you will need to take a stand, to convince your readers of a particular point of view. Though you must present opposing views fairly, you should clearly state your own view and the evidence to support that view. Your readers will expect you to take one side and to argue reasonably that your view is better or stronger than other views. (See A2 in *A Writer's Reference*.) Here is an example of a paragraph that was revised to stay focused on one side of an issue.

ORIGINAL: DOES NOT TAKE A STAND

Most experts in the United States agree that spanking is not an appropriate form of discipline for children. Some people, however, feel that spanking is acceptable because it can correct behavioral problems such as back-talking. Spanking may lead to larger problems of fear and anxiety. Many children experience no lasting emotional problems from it. Opinions differ on this controversial topic.

REVISED: TAKES A STAND

Most experts in the United States agree that spanking is not an appropriate form of discipline for children. Spanking may temporarily correct a behavioral problem such as back-talking, but it may lead to larger problems such as increased aggression, and it may teach children that violence is an acceptable means of getting what they want ("Guidance" 726). Spanking should be used sparingly as a discipline option.

The original version does not take a stand on the issue of spanking. It only points out that there are differing views on the subject. In the revision, the writer takes a position and uses expert opinion (an article from the journal of the American Academy of Pediatrics) for support.

H3-c Include details that support the main idea directly.

Like busy professionals taking a taxi to the airport, academic readers in the United States prefer that you take the most direct route to your destination, with no detours along the way. They expect your writing to stay focused, each sentence supporting the main point of its paragraph. Your writing should include details, of course, but each detail should directly support your main point. Otherwise readers may think that you have lost your focus or are wasting their time.

If you are accustomed to a writing style that often includes details that are interesting or thought-provoking but not *directly* related to the main idea, you may have a difficult time identifying the difference between necessary and unnecessary details. To recognize what academic English readers consider necessary details, try reading student papers that are considered effective models of academic writing. Often the best way to improve your own writing skills is to review several models.

ON THE WEB > dianahacker.com/writersref
Model papers

In the following paragraph, the writer wanders off the topic (see the highlighted sentence). In the revision, each detail supports the main idea of the paragraph and there are no unnecessary details.

PARAGRAPH WITH UNNECESSARY DETAILS

The gray wolf may not be as harmful to cattle ranching as some believe. Many residents of the western United States are opposed to allowing the gray wolf into western wilderness areas because they believe that the wolves will kill ranchers' herds and ruin their businesses. However, in the last few years, very few cows have been killed by wolves, while thousands of cows have been killed by lightning, storms, and other animals, including coyotes. Although the coyote is related to the wolf and inhabits the same areas, it is lighter in color and smaller in size. While wolves may cause some economic losses, to say that wolves alone will ruin the ranching business overstates the animals' actual impact.

FOCUSED PARAGRAPH

The gray wolf may not be as harmful to cattle ranching as some believe. Many residents of the western United States are opposed to allowing the gray wolf into western wilderness areas because they believe that the wolves will kill ranchers' herds and ruin their businesses. However, in the last few years, very few cows have been killed by wolves, while thousands of cows have been killed by lightning, storms, and other animals, including coyotes. While wolves may cause some economic losses, to say that wolves alone will ruin the ranching business overstates the animals' actual impact.

H3-d Learn to recognize intellectual property and avoid accidental plagiarism.

In some cultures, copying and memorizing texts is a highly valued activity. Using the exact words of scholars in your own writing can be a way of honoring what those scholars have said. In the United States, however, the exact language, images, and original ideas contained in any published work are considered *intellectual property*, which is protected as if it were physical property.

In an academic paper, you are expected to incorporate information and ideas from your sources into your writing. That source material is the intellectual property of its author or publisher, and you must acknowledge your use of that property by following standard academic practices, referred to as *citing your sources* (see R3-c and MLA-2, APA-2, and CMS-2 in *A Writer's Reference*). Even if you do not intend to cheat or steal, you commit a type of theft known as *plagiarism* if you do not properly cite your sources.

Recognizing intellectual property

Recognizing intellectual property can be difficult if you are still becoming accustomed to using the English language. The chart on page H-26 can help you determine whether an idea you have included in your paper is someone else's intellectual property. If you encounter an idea that you think might be intellectual property but is not mentioned in the chart, take a draft of your paper to your instructor or your school's writing center. It is important that you catch cases of accidental plagiarism before you turn in your work.

Avoiding plagiarism by integrating and citing sources

When you use another writer's words or ideas, you must treat that material according to standard academic conventions in the text of your paper, a process called *integrating sources*. The chart on page H-28 will help you determine how to integrate and cite your sources to avoid plagiarism. The examples in the chart are given in MLA style. For more on integrating and citing sources in MLA style, see MLA-2 and MLA-3 in *A Writer's Reference*. For information on APA and CMS styles, see APA-2 and APA-3 and CMS-2 and CMS-3, respectively.

You also must provide a list of your sources at the end of your paper (the list is called Works Cited in MLA, References in APA, and Bibliography in CMS). For details, see MLA-4, APA-4, and CMS-4.

Recognizing intellectual property

Intellectual property

The first column shows the types of information that are considered intellectual property. The second column gives an example from a student essay using and citing a source with the MLA style of documentation (used in English and some humanities). See MLA-4 in *A Writer's Reference* for complete details about citing sources in the text of your paper and in the list of works cited at the end. See APA-4 for details about citation in the social sciences, and see CMS-4 for details about citation in history and other humanities.

TYPE OF INFORMATION	EXAMPLES WITH APPROPRIATE CITATIONS
Any *exact* words from a published source (even if the source provides a fact)	**IN-TEXT CITATION** Luis N. Rivera writes, "Five hundred years ago, thanks to the nautical audacity and cosmographical ignorance of an Italian mariner . . . the Atlantic Ocean ceased to be a divider and became the waterway connection between Europe, Africa, and the Americas" (270). **WORKS CITED ENTRY** Rivera, Luis N. A Violent Evangelism. Louisville: Westminster, 1992.
Any original ideas from a published source—even if you've paraphrased the source (written the information in your own words)	**IN-TEXT CITATION** Historian Paul Gordon Lauren shows that even though the First World War did not seem to be about race at first, a number of racial issues had surfaced by the time the war ended in 1918 (75). **WORKS CITED ENTRY** Lauren, Paul Gordon. Power and Prejudice. 2nd ed. Boulder: Westview, 1996.
Results of a study	**IN-TEXT CITATION** One study showed that cutting down trees that have been burned in forest fires prevents new trees from growing in the area (Donato et al. 352). **WORKS CITED ENTRY** Donato, D. C., et al. "Post-Wildfire Logging Hinders Regeneration and Increases Fire Risk." Science 311 (2006): 352.

Statistics

IN-TEXT CITATION

Gore writes, "In 1988, the EPA reported that the ground water in thirty-two states was contaminated with seventy-four different agricultural chemicals, including one, herbicide atrazine, that is classified as a potential human carcinogen" (xxii-xxiii).

WORKS CITED ENTRY

Gore, Al. Introduction. Silent Spring. By Rachel Carson. Boston: Houghton, 1994. xv-xxvi.

Theories

IN-TEXT CITATION

While many linguists have argued that language is a "cultural invention," Steven Pinker claims that language is an "instinct"; he writes that it is "not a cultural artifact" but "a distinct piece of the biological makeup of our brains" (4).

WORKS CITED ENTRY

Pinker, Steven. The Language Instinct. New York: Perennial, 2000.

Not intellectual property

The first column shows the types of information that are *not* considered intellectual property and that may be used in a paper without citing a source. The second column gives examples of each type.

TYPE OF INFORMATION	EXAMPLES
Well-known historical, scientific, or cultural facts	Christopher Columbus sailed across the Atlantic Ocean in 1492.
	World War I ended in 1918.
	Forest fires are sometimes caused by lightning.
	Rachel Carson wrote Silent Spring.
Broad, general observations	Many languages are spoken in the United States.
	Some students tend to have more motivation than others.
	Many US residents own cars and computers.

NOTE: For types of information not on this list, check with your instructor or your school's writing center to determine whether you need to cite the source. When in doubt, you are always safe to cite the source.

Integrating and citing sources to avoid plagiarism

SOURCE TEXT

Our language is constantly changing. Like the Mississippi, it keeps forging new channels and abandoning old ones, picking up debris, depositing unwanted silt, and frequently bursting its banks. In every generation, there are people who deplore changes in the language and many who wish to stop the flow. But if our language stopped changing it would mean that American society had ceased to be dynamic, innovative, pulsing with life—that the river had frozen up.

—Robert MacNeil and William Cran,
Do You Speak American?, p. 1

NOTE: The examples in this chart follow MLA style (see MLA-4 in *A Writer's Reference*). For information on APA and CMS styles, see APA-4 and CMS-4, respectively.

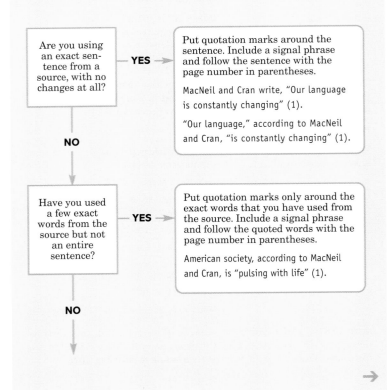

Are you using an exact sentence from a source, with no changes at all? **YES** → Put quotation marks around the sentence. Include a signal phrase and follow the sentence with the page number in parentheses.

MacNeil and Cran write, "Our language is constantly changing" (1).

"Our language," according to MacNeil and Cran, "is constantly changing" (1).

NO

Have you used a few exact words from the source but not an entire sentence? **YES** → Put quotation marks only around the exact words that you have used from the source. Include a signal phrase and follow the quoted words with the page number in parentheses.

American society, according to MacNeil and Cran, is "pulsing with life" (1).

NO

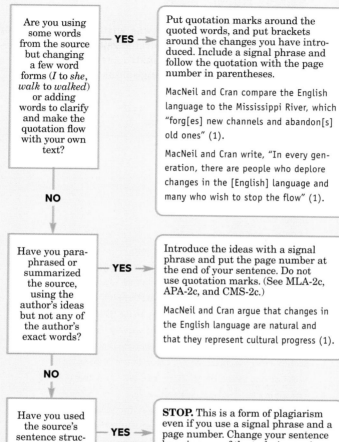

Are you using some words from the source but changing a few word forms (*I* to *she*, *walk* to *walked*) or adding words to clarify and make the quotation flow with your own text?

YES → Put quotation marks around the quoted words, and put brackets around the changes you have introduced. Include a signal phrase and follow the quotation with the page number in parentheses.

MacNeil and Cran compare the English language to the Mississippi River, which "forg[es] new channels and abandon[s] old ones" (1).

MacNeil and Cran write, "In every generation, there are people who deplore changes in the [English] language and many who wish to stop the flow" (1).

NO ↓

Have you paraphrased or summarized the source, using the author's ideas but not any of the author's exact words?

YES → Introduce the ideas with a signal phrase and put the page number at the end of your sentence. Do not use quotation marks. (See MLA-2c, APA-2c, and CMS-2c.)

MacNeil and Cran argue that changes in the English language are natural and that they represent cultural progress (1).

NO ↓

Have you used the source's sentence structure but substituted a few synonyms for the author's words?

YES → **STOP.** This is a form of plagiarism even if you use a signal phrase and a page number. Change your sentence by using one of the techniques given in this chart or in MLA-3, APA-3, or CMS-3.

PLAGIARIZED

MacNeil and Cran claim that, like a river, English creates new waterways and discards old ones.

INTEGRATED AND CITED CORRECTLY

MacNeil and Cran claim, "Like the Mississippi, [English] keeps forging new channels and abandoning old ones" (1).

H3-e Sample student essay

The following brief argument paper was written by Amy Zhang, a student in a composition class. The first version (pp. H-30 to H-32) shows Zhang's initial draft with her instructor's comments. The second version (pp. H-33 to H-36) is Zhang's final draft.

ROUGH DRAFT, WITH INSTRUCTOR'S COMMENTS

Zhang 1

Amy Zhang

Professor Swain

English 101

16 October 2006

The Importance of Food

Title needs to be more focused. A clearer thesis in first paragraph may help.

Drive on any highway in America and you'll find fast-food restau-

Missing article (E3-c)

rants at every exit and service area. Walk through any supermarket and you'll see prepared foods that say "make it in minutes" and "ready to serve." According to article by James Bone on the TimesOnline Web site, only one-third of Americans cook meals from scratch, meaning with fresh ingredients. Bone also report that Americans spend only thirty minutes cooking dinner, compared with 2-1/2 hours in the 1960s. And in his book Fast Food Nation, Eric Schlosser claims that one-quarter of Americans eat in a fast-food restaurant each day (3).

Verb tense (E1-a)

Opening paragraph needs a clear thesis. (C2-a)

Missing article with proper noun (E3-g)

In most households in United States, two people are working (Bone), and people with full-time jobs have little time for food shopping and cooking meals. Instead of coming home from work at night and chopping vegetables, many people prefer to cook something in their microwave or get take-out from a chain restaurant. This is why Americans are eating fast food so often--they don't have enough time.

This sentence sounds like the main point of the paragraph. Try moving it to beginning of paragraph. (H3-a)

And even if Americans did have more time to cook every night, it is hard for them to find good food anywhere. Modern agriculture, which is focused on disease resistance, long shelf life, and shippability, has sacrificed taste. Supermarkets devote far more space to boxed and canned items than they do to frozen foods and fresh meat, fish, and vegetables.

Paragraph strays from main topic of paper. Consider eliminating. (H3-c)

Zhang 2

Another reason that mealtime has become so short is that many younger adults grew up in what one might call a fast-food culture. In the past thirty years, inventions such as cell phone, fax machine, and computer have increased the pace of life. At the same time, microwave oven, drive-through restaurant, and TV dinner have changed the way Americans eat. Many people now prefer to eat quickly, even in their cars or in front of the television, instead of take time to cook a meal and sit at the table. In this culture of instant gratification, people don't think food is important enough to spend much time on.

Noun ("-ing" form) after preposition (E5-b)

Plural nouns for general categories (E3-f)

Americans' obsession with fast food has caused the quality of their lives to go down. First of all, their health is suffering. As most people know, fast foods and frozen meals generally less healthy than foods made from scratch. They have lots of preservatives, fat, sugar, and salt to hide the fact that they are not fresh. If people will not eat fresh foods that provide necessary vitamins and minerals, they may become tired and sick, and they may miss out on opportunities to enjoy their lives.

Missing linking verb (E2-a)

No "will" in "if" clause (E1-e)

Possible plagiarism. Check the source. If the words are directly from the source, use quotation marks. (H3-d)

Another serious health concern is obesity. Is an obesity epidemic in America today, especially with young people, that is related to the way people are eating. According to Schlosser, "the rate of obesity among American children is twice as high as it was in the late 1970s" (240). Obesity can lead to many health problems, including diabetes, heart disease, and cancer. The United States Department of Health and Human Services notes that deaths due to poor diet and physical inactivity increased 33 percent over the past decade and may soon overtake tobacco as the leading cause of death in this country. Certainly, if fast food causes people to become obese, and then obesity causes them to get sick or die, fast food cannot be consider an "improvement" in Americans' lives.

Place-holder "There" missing (E2-b)

End of essay needs development.

Passive verb form (E1-c)

The economy causes most people to work long hours, and that leaves little time for cooking, so it is understandable that people rely so much on fast food. It makes life much easier and allows parents to get other things done around the house and spend time with their children. If they try hard enough, people can even find healthy options at fast-food restaurants, such as salads and bottled water instead of fries and sodas. So maybe fast food isn't always a bad thing.

This para-graph may confuse readers--it takes the opposite view of your main point. Revise to acknowledge opposing view without contradicting your main point. (H3-b)

Readers expect a strong ending with a clear point, not an open-ended statement.

Zhang 3

Works Cited

For an online source, include the URL in your citation.

Bone, James. "Good Home Cooking--Right off the Assembly
        Line." TimesOnline 27 Mar. 2006. 9 Oct. 2006.

Schlosser, Eric. Fast Food Nation: The Dark Side of the All-American
        Meal. Boston: Houghton, 2001.

United States. Dept. of Health and Human Services. "Citing
        'Dangerous Increase' in Deaths, HHS Launches New Strategies
        against Overweight Epidemic." 9 Mar. 2004. 9 Oct. 2006
        <http://www.hhs.gov/news/press/2004pres/20040309.html>.

FINAL DRAFT

Zhang 1

Amy Zhang

Professor Swain

English 101

23 October 2006

Slow Down and Eat Better

Drive on any highway in America and you'll find fast-food restaurants at every exit and service area. Walk through any supermarket and
you'll see prepared foods that say "make it in minutes" and "ready to
serve." According to an article by James Bone on the TimesOnline Web
site, only one-third of Americans cook meals from scratch, meaning with
fresh ingredients. Bone also reports that Americans spend only thirty
minutes cooking dinner, compared with 2-1/2 hours in the 1960s. And in
his book Fast Food Nation, Eric Schlosser claims that one-quarter of
Americans eat in a fast-food restaurant each day (3). Why are Americans
eating so much fast food? The answer is simple: they are willing to trade
quality for speed. While Americans may be attracted to food that is fast
and easy, they are missing some important benefits of slowing down. In
fact, Americans' obsession with fast food is hurting not only their health
but also the quality of their lives.

The main reason that Americans are getting take-out food and
cooking prepared meals is obvious: they don't have enough time. In
more than two-thirds of households in America, two people are working
(Bone). People with demanding work schedules have little time for food
shopping and cooking.

Another reason that mealtime has become so short is that many
younger adults grew up in what one might call a fast-food culture. In the
past fifty years, inventions such as televisions, fax machines, and com-
puters have increased the pace of life. At the same time, microwave
ovens, drive-through restaurants, and TV dinners have changed the way
Americans eat. Many people now prefer to eat quickly, even in their cars
or in front of the television, instead of taking time to cook a meal and
sit at the table. In this culture of instant gratification, people don't
think food is important enough to spend much time on.

Even though Americans think that they are saving time and im-

Zhang opens
with general
observations to
attract readers'
interest.

Zhang states a
clear thesis at
the end of
the opening
paragraph.

Clear topic
sentence helps
guide readers.

Effective transition links
ideas in this paragraph
to those in the previous
paragraph.

Marginal annotations indicate MLA-style formatting and effective writing.

proving their lives by eating precooked and prepackaged food, their obsession with fast food is causing the quality of their lives to go down. First, their health is suffering. As most people know, fast foods and frozen meals are generally less healthy than foods made from scratch. They have lots of preservatives, fat, sugar, and salt to hide the fact that they are not fresh. When people do not eat fresh foods that provide necessary vitamins and minerals, they may become tired and sick, and they will miss out on opportunities to enjoy their lives.

Another serious health concern is obesity. There is an obesity epidemic in America today, especially with young people, that is related to the way people are eating. According to Schlosser, "the rate of obesity among American children is twice as high as it was in the late 1970s" (240). Obesity can lead to many health problems, including diabetes, heart disease, and cancer. The United States Department of Health and Human Services notes that "deaths due to poor diet and physical inactivity increased 33 percent" over the past decade and it cites a study concluding that "poor diet and physical inactivity may soon overtake tobacco as the leading cause of death" in this country. Certainly, if fast food causes people to become obese, and then obesity causes them to get sick or die, fast food cannot be considered an "improvement" in Americans' lives.

In addition to making health problems, fast food hurts people's relationships with their friends and families. In an online interview, John Robbins, author of Diet for a New America and The Food Revolution, comments on the importance of mealtime:

> Throughout history, eating has been a way of bringing people together. It's how parents stay in touch with what's going on in their kids' lives. When people break bread together, it's an act of peacemaking, an act of good will. . . . Dining together can be a deep biological and sacred experience. When we eat, we are connected to all of life. It's a phenomenon found in every culture in the world, except ours. I see the McDonaldization of our food supply as the annihilation of our true relationship to life.

Zhang uses a signal phrase and a parenthetical citation for facts that support her thesis.

No page number is available for this online source.

A long quotation (more than four lines) is indented; quotation marks are omitted. An ellipsis mark indicates that some words from the source have been left out.

Zhang 3

While most Americans will not be able to cook full, fresh meals every day, they can begin to improve the quality of their lives by buying fresh foods when there is an option and by cooking fresh food at least occasionally. For example, people can shop at the farmers' market for fresh local produce instead of buying canned or frozen products. They not only will have a chance to buy foods with more nutrients but also will have the chance to get to know people in their community.

Also, if people slow down to make food with their friends or family, they can enjoy the benefits of good nutrition while they are building stronger relationships. On its Web site, Slow Food, which describes itself as "an international organization whose aim is to protect the pleasures of the table from the homogenization of modern fast food and life," encourages people to make pasta from scratch once in a while. Friends and family can cook meals together so one person isn't doing all the work. And people can try to cook old family recipes the way their grandparents did.

Even though Americans may think they are saving time and improving their lives by eating fast food, they will actually have healthier and more enjoyable lives if they change the way they cook and eat. Making dinner from scratch is much healthier than getting burgers and fries from a fast-food restaurant. And people get more than just a full stomach--they get more time with family and friends and a good feeling from creating something healthy.

Zhang acknowledges the limitations of her argument while maintaining her position.

Zhang offers readers some suggestions for better eating.

Conclusion reminds readers of the essay's main point.

Zhang 4

The works cited list provides references for all the sources Zhang uses in her paper.

Works Cited

Bone, James. "Good Home Cooking--Right off the Assembly
    Line." TimesOnline 27 Mar. 2006. 9 Oct. 2006
    <http://www.timesonline.co.uk/article/
    0,,11069-2105427,00.html>.

Robbins, John. "The Common Ground Interview with John
    Robbins." The Food Revolution. 2002. 18 Oct. 2006
    <http://www.foodrevolution.org/commonground.htm>.

Schlosser, Eric. Fast Food Nation: The Dark Side of the All-American
    Meal. Boston: Houghton, 2001.

Slow Food. Slowfood.com. 18 Oct. 2006 <http://www.slowfood.com>.

United States. Dept. of Health and Human Services. "Citing
    'Dangerous Increase' in Deaths, HHS Launches New Strategies
    against Overweight Epidemic." 9 Mar. 2004. 9 Oct. 2006
    <http://www.hhs.gov/news/press/2004pres/20040309.html>.

H4

Practice exercises

This section includes both intensive and extensive grammar and writing exercises. The intensive activities will help you focus on specific areas of grammar such as verb tense and use of articles. The extensive activities will help build your English fluency—your ability to use English quickly and easily without hesitating or translating from your native language.

H4-a Intensive grammar exercises

The intensive exercises in this section can help you improve your awareness and proper use of the English grammar covered in the tabbed section E of *A Writer's Reference*, Sixth Edition. These exercises will also help you strengthen your editing skills when you edit your own writing in English. (For help building fluency rather than grammar and editing skills, see the extensive writing practices in H4-b, starting on p. H-46.) Answers to all the exercises appear at the end of this section.

EXERCISE H1–1 Verb forms and tenses Edit the following sentences to correct errors in verb forms and verb tenses. If a sentence is correct, write "correct" after it. (For help, see E1-a in *A Writer's Reference*. You may need to refer to G2-a for help with irregular verbs.) Example:

> *moved*
> I ~~move~~ to Florida three years ago.
> ^

1. When she got home, Mina realize that she had forgotten to buy staples while she was out.
2. Martin Luther King Jr., the famous orator and civil rights activist, deliver his famous "I Have a Dream" speech on August 28, 1963.
3. David was playing soccer for the last fifteen years.
4. Mangoes, which originally grew only in Asia, now grew in the Eastern and Western Hemispheres.
5. Anders has already read *To Kill a Mockingbird* three times.
6. Alexander Fleming discovered penicillin while he was worked at a hospital in London.
7. Moving to a new country often cause people to change their lifestyles.

8. Although anthropologists do not know exactly when the first calendar was invented, they have evidence that solar calendars are existing for at least six thousand years.
9. When they moved here, my husband and his brother open a small restaurant.
10. Professors in the United States often requiring their students to work in groups.

EXERCISE H1–2 **Verb forms and tenses**   Edit the following sentences to correct errors in verb forms and verb tenses. If a sentence is correct, write "correct" after it. (For help, see E1-a in *A Writer's Reference*. You may need to refer to G2-a for help with irregular verbs.) Example:

loved
Amy ~~was loving~~ Woody Guthrie's songs when she was a child.
^

1. Woody Guthrie was being one of the best-known American folk singer–activists.
2. Born in 1912, Guthrie spend his early life surrounded by music in his small hometown of Okema, Oklahoma.
3. Before his twentieth birthday, he was moving to Texas, where he attempted to start a career as a musician.
4. While Guthrie was in Texas, a decade-long period of dust storms began sweeping through the central United States.
5. Guthrie and his family move west to California along with many other Texans and Oklahomans who found employment as farmworkers.
6. While he was traveled, he was exposed to the harsh treatment the migrant workers received.
7. By the time Guthrie arrive in California, he had developed a deep sense of resentment for the rich owners who exploited poor farmworkers.
8. He begin writing and singing more songs about workers' rights and political protest, including his most famous song, "This Land Is Your Land."
9. He continued writing songs with a political edge for the rest of his life and motivate many other popular folk and rock singers to carry on his legacy.
10. Today, Guthrie's music live on in younger generations of people who feel inspired by his words.

EXERCISE H1–3 **Verb forms and tenses**   Edit the following paragraph to correct errors in verb forms and verb tenses. There are ten errors. (For help, see E1-a in *A Writer's Reference*. You may need to refer to G2-a for help with irregular verbs.)

Since I have been only eight years old, I have dream of becoming a professional baseball player. Trying to develop the skill of a professional player has been both physically and mentally challenging. One of the greatest difficulties that I have face is fear. When I become the pitcher on my high school team, I was under a lot of pressure; my teammates, coach, and all the students at my school depended on me to win games. The thought of losing terrify me. Before a few games in my first season, I have put so much pressure on myself to win and to be a good leader that I freezed. In time, though, I learn to manage my stress and to make the fear work in my favor. By the time I was a senior, I was transforming the fear into energy that helped me stay alert and quick. Although I know I will have many more challenges to face in pursuit of my dream, I am confident that someday I succeed.

EXERCISE H1–4 Modal verbs In the following dialogue, choose the correct modal verb or verb phrase in parentheses. (For help, see E1-b in *A Writer's Reference*.)

> **HALEY:** Good morning, Professor Weil. (May / Would) I ask you for some advice about my course work?
>
> **PROFESSOR WEIL:** Sure, Haley. What (can / will) I help you with?
>
> **H:** I (will / would) like to change my major. I'm enrolled as a biology major now, but I am not as interested in science as I thought I (will be / would be).
>
> **P:** I see. What major are you thinking of?
>
> **H:** Since I am very good at math, I think I would like to be a business major.
>
> **P:** That's a good idea, but (can / may) you do well in classes that don't involve math?
>
> **H:** I think so. Which courses (must I to take / must I take) besides math?
>
> **P:** You will have to take some communications and writing courses.
>
> **H:** I (can do / can to do) that. I will go to the registrar and select my courses. Thank you, Professor Weil!

EXERCISE H1–5 Passive verb forms Edit the following paragraph to correct errors in passive verb forms. There are ten errors. (For help, see E1-c in *A Writer's Reference*. You may need to refer to G2-a for help with irregular verbs.)

> Most people think of a trash bin as a finishing point rather than a starting point. However, a recycling bin can be the start of a new life for a piece of paper. After paper is put into an office bin, it is ship to a

recycling center, where it is sorting into types: office paper, cardboard, or colored paper. After it is sorted, it is sended to a paper mill, where it is chop into dry pulp. The pulp is then mixed with water to form a wet substance called "slurry." The slurry is sent through a screen, which removes little bits of excess materials such as glue, plastic, or staples. After it goes through the screen, the slurry is rinse again to remove inks. Then the slurry goes through a machine that makes the paper fibers grow bigger. Next the slurry is water down and place on a screen, where it is press into long, thin sheets and dried on heated rollers. The dried sheets are rolling up and shipped off to other companies where they are process and made into the paper products we use every day.

EXERCISE H1–6 Negative verb forms Edit the following sentences to correct errors in the use of negative verb forms. (For help, see E1-d in *A Writer's Reference*.) Example:

> Even though I was tired, I could ~~no~~ sleep.
> _{not}

1. If the governor is reelected, she not will raise the income tax.
2. I could no park my car next to the library because all of the spaces were taken.
3. Sadly, a cure for AIDS has no been found yet.
4. The book that we have to buy for our ecology class not is very expensive.
5. I tried to make a photocopy, but the copier was no functioning properly.
6. Sunnie did not came with us to the football game last Saturday.
7. Although Omar not like to drive in traffic, he likes to race cars on the weekends.
8. Snow leopards no are extinct, but they are on the endangered species list.
9. Kim could not find no lychees at the supermarket because they are not very common in the United States.
10. I was disappointed that I didn't knew the woman's name.

EXERCISE H1–7 Conditional sentences Edit the following conditional sentences to correct any problems with verbs. If a sentence is correct, write "correct" after it. (For help, see E1-e in *A Writer's Reference*.) Example:

> If the Chargers ~~will~~ win the game tonight, they will move on to the
>
> district finals.

1. If Deborah arrived earlier, she might have found a better parking space.
2. I'll buy you a soda if you will come to the cafeteria with me.
3. The city will not increase the sales tax unless the citizens vote in favor of the new tax law.

4. Most scientists think that if the world does not reduce carbon dioxide emissions, global warming will occur.
5. If I was a famous actor, I would move to Bel Aire and buy a mansion.
6. If you will use aloe on a burn, you can reduce the chances of developing a scar.
7. You would have to pay late charges if you don't return your rental video on time.
8. Unless the Security Council will agree, the UN will not send peace-keeping troops to war-torn countries.
9. When Rosa left for college every September, she closes her summer gardening business.
10. If Kevin would be here with us today, he would be enjoying himself.

EXERCISE H1–8 Verbs followed by gerunds or infinitives Edit the following paragraph to correct problems with verbs followed by gerunds or infinitives. There are eight errors. (For help, see E1-f in *A Writer's Reference*.)

When I was young, my family and I went on an annual camping trip in the canyons of the southwestern United States. One summer, I convinced my family taking a tour of several canyons: the Grand Canyon, Bryce Canyon, and Canyonlands National Park. I remember to be amazed at each stop along the way. I loved looking up at the twisting towers of red rock, wondering how they had avoided to fall down in the last several thousand years. (I can recall to think that some might fall over if someone in the canyon sneezed a little too hard.) Even at that young age, I sensed the power of these remarkable landmarks and understood the spell that they had held over so many generations of residents and visitors. In my heart, I promised going back to the canyons every year. Though I never planned giving up my promise, the commitments of adulthood have prevented me from taking annual trips back to the canyons. I miss to visit the red rocks on a regular basis, but I still manage going back to the Southwest every few years. Breathing in the high desert air while gazing up at the red rock towers never ceases to refresh and rejuvenate me.

EXERCISE H2–1 Linking verbs Add linking verbs where necessary in the following paragraphs. There are seven missing verbs. (For help, see E2-a in *A Writer's Reference*.)

When I only a boy, I was known for being lazy. Every time my parents asked me to clean my room or study for my classes, I always found an excuse to avoid the work. Sometimes I would pretend that I too tired; other times I would pretend that I had simply forgotten their request. Most of the time, however, I would try to approach the situation logically, arguing that since my older brother stronger and had more life experience, he should be responsible for most of the household chores.

However, when I started college, my life changed. I realized that
in order to become the successful college student I wanted to be, I
would have to take control of my life, change my bad habits, and act responsibly. Now I no longer the lazy boy my parents knew when I was a
child. I wake up early, exercise, and go to school. I never late to my
classes, and I always turn my assignments in on time. Although I still
far from perfect, I try to help others whenever I can. Whenever someone needs me, particularly at school or at home, I never try to hide as I
did when I just a boy.

EXERCISE H2–2 Missing subjects Five sentences in the following paragraph are missing subjects. Add them where they are needed. (For help, see
E2-b in *A Writer's Reference.*)

Is common to think that being the oldest child in a family has the
most privileges. However, are several advantages to being the youngest
child, too. First, is important to note that by the time the youngest
child is born, the parents have already had experience as parents. They
know how to care for a newborn, and they tend to be more relaxed. Second, the youngest child has the opportunity to learn how to stay out of
trouble. If the older children get into trouble, is easy for the youngest
child to learn from the older children's mistakes. A third advantage of
being the youngest child is that in many cases, the youngest gets extra
attention from the older siblings. Is not unusual to see older siblings
taking care of their younger siblings at school or protecting them from
bullies.

EXERCISE H2–3 Unnecessary words Edit the following sentences by
deleting unnecessary words. (In some cases, more than one correction is possible.) If a sentence is correct, write "correct" after it. (For help, see E2-c,
E2-d, and E2-e in *A Writer's Reference.*) Example:

> *the food*
> ~~The food~~ I ate ~~it~~ very quickly.
>   ^

1. Coming to the United States it changed more than my address. It
   changed the direction of my career.
2. My life here in Gainesville it's different from the life that I lived in
   Bolivia.
3. When I was in Bolivia, I was a chef.
4. I attended a culinary school, which it was the best in Bolivia, and I was
   offered the chance to study for a short time in the United States.
5. When I first came, I met other students who they had different majors.
6. I learned many things from my roommate, Jin, who was a business
   major.
7. Jin he helped me realize the importance of having business experience.

8. I learned that although I enjoyed being a chef, but I didn't want to be a chef without business knowledge.
9. I decided to stay a bit longer in the United States, where I could study international business here.
10. Someday I will combine both interests and start my own chain of specialized restaurants, which I hope to build them all over the world.

EXERCISE H2–4 Placement of adverbs   Edit the following sentences to put adverbs in their proper place. If a sentence is correct, write "correct" after it. (For help, see E2-f in *A Writer's Reference*.) Example:

My roommate likes to play ~~very loudly~~ the drums/ *very loudly.*

1. I have never seen a player hit so hard a baseball.
2. Sue cooked very slowly the soup so that the vegetables would be tender.
3. Regular study habits can help students complete all their assignments efficiently.
4. After I finished my workout, I stretched carefully my tender muscles.
5. The professor seemed surprised that the class finished so quickly the exam.
6. After I read the user manual, I installed easily the new hard drive.
7. My mother always told me that she loved equally all her children.
8. As soon as I got the keys to my new car, I drove everywhere my friends.
9. The government found out that the company manufactured illegally the drug.
10. Although she had a difficult time in the past, this year she won very easily the gold medal in cross-country skiing.

EXERCISE H3–1 Articles   Edit the following sentences to correct errors in the use of articles (*a, an, the*). (For help, see E3 in *A Writer's Reference*.) Example:

a
Holly recently bought new sound system for her car.

1. When people move to new place, they definitely have to go through some changes.
2. Temperature dropped twenty degrees in a half hour yesterday.
3. Some governments help couples who have more than two children by giving them the health insurance.
4. When people are too busy, they sometimes forget to eat the dinner.
5. Students are exposed to the new experiences when they move to a new country.
6. I chose to have small family so that I could give my children sufficient attention.

7. Marco became more familiar with the nature when he studied in the rain forests of Brazil.
8. Let me give you an advice: Buy your books early.
9. A common effect of culture shock is the loneliness.
10. Because our school doesn't allow cars within the campus gates, I walk from my parking spot to place where I need to go.

EXERCISE H3–2 Articles   Edit the following paragraph to correct errors in the use of articles (*a, an, the*). There are ten errors. (For help, see E3 in *A Writer's Reference*.)

Heifer International is nonprofit organization that provides the animals to poor farmers and families around world. Organization was started in 1940s by man named Dan West, relief worker who gave people food during times of crisis. West realized that he could help people even more by giving them animals that could supply food— such as the milk and cheese— for several years. He wanted to help people for the long term, and he wanted to help them have the pride in themselves. Now Heifer serves communities in more than one hundred countries around world. Its mission is to help families by providing some animals that the families can use to support themselves or start small businesses.

EXERCISE H3–3 Articles   Edit the following sentences to correct errors in the use of articles (*a, an, the*). In some cases, more than one revision is possible. (For help, see E3 in *A Writer's Reference*.)

A greeting is the way that the person addresses or acknowledges another person when the two meet. Types of greetings vary in different countries. People in the Japan often prefer to greet nonverbally, with bow and a smile. African would likely greet fellow African with the handshake. For the Maori people of New Zealand, a most common greeting is the *hongi*, which involves rubbing noses. In Poland, kiss on each cheek is customary; but the Dutch custom is to kiss the right cheek, then the left, and then the right again. Traveler to another country would be wise to learn greetings expected by its people.

EXERCISE H4–1 Present and past participles   Choose the correct participle in the parentheses in the following sentences. (For help, see E4 in *A Writer's Reference*.) Example:

My (tiring / tired) old dog sleeps all day.

1. Charlie thinks I'm (confusing / confused). He says that he doesn't understand me because I talk too fast and never stop to explain my thoughts.

2. My feet still hurt from the long, (tiring / tired) walk we took yesterday.
3. Alex and her boyfriend went to see a really (boring / bored) movie last night.
4. Myrna is always busy. She's a (working / worked) mom with three kids — and she goes to college!
5. Gavin said that Professor Snyder's mythology lecture was (fascinating / fascinated).
6. Is your essay (handwriting / handwritten), or is it (typing / typed)?
7. I will be (satisfying / satisfied) if I can read at least two chapters in my chemistry text over the weekend.
8. This vase is beautiful! Is it (hand-painting / hand-painted)?
9. The commercial claims that this (cleaning / cleaned) product helps kill bacteria.
10. Señora Quiroga put two cups of (peeling / peeled) apples in the bowl.

EXERCISES H5–1 Prepositions showing time and place Edit the following sentences to correct the use of prepositions. If a sentence is correct, write "correct" after it. (For help, see E5-a in *A Writer's Reference*.) Example:

on
The office will be closed ~~at~~ Memorial Day.
　　　　　　　　　　　　　^

1. Does your dance class start in Monday or Wednesday?
2. Fran was working at her desk when the earthquake hit.
3. As soon as Fiona moved into her dorm room, she put a poster of Einstein in the wall for inspiration.
4. My books are a little dusty because they were packed away on the garage for a year.
5. Dr. Horn is taking his students to Ghana for a study trip on early June.
6. My grandmother was born at Los Angeles, but my grandfather was born at Albuquerque.
7. My fraternity brothers like to play loud music at the street in front of our building.
8. My exam begins at two hours, but I'm not nervous at all.
9. Did you read the essay in *The Bedford Reader*, or were you able to find it on the Internet?
10. Bret finished writing his term paper right on midnight.

EXERCISE H5–2 Preposition combinations Edit the following sentences for errors in preposition combinations (preposition + noun, adjective + preposition, or verb + preposition). If a sentence is correct, write "correct" after it. (For help, see E5-b, E5-c, and E5-d in *A Writer's Reference*.) Example:

about
Sandra has been dreaming ~~with~~ becoming a doctor.
　　　　　　　　　　　　　　　　^

1. I have trouble concentrating in my homework when my roommate is around.

2. The senator was skilled at delay controversial votes.
3. I'm not worried with our verbs test on Wednesday.
4. While Ellie proofread the group's report, Sam and Tomi worked in the presentation slides.
5. The executives were found guilty of insider trading.
6. The solution consists in sodium and water.
7. I was afraid to board the plane because I'm not accustomed with traveling alone.
8. Shea remained devoted on the teachings of his martial arts master.
9. You can always count with Carole to help out when the office gets busy.
10. Iona wasn't aware of the trouble the manager was experiencing.

H4-b Topics for writing practice

The writing prompts beginning on page H-47 can help you build fluency and confidence in using English grammar in academic situations. Use the prompts in conjunction with the intensive and extensive practice instructions on this page and the next. If you would like to focus on points of grammar, sentence structure, essay development, or editing skills, use the directions for intensive practice. If you would like to develop your fluency— your ability to write in English without translating from your native language— use the directions for extensive practice. Each prompt is accompanied by a suggested writing focus, which can be used with either the intensive or the extensive practice.

Directions for intensive practice (focus on grammar and on writing and editing skills)

1. Write a paragraph or an essay on one of the prompts beginning on page H-47.
2. Edit and revise your work carefully, paying attention to the suggested writing focus (or any other focus your instructor recommends).
3. Take your finished work to your instructor or to the writing center for a conference. If you take your work to the writing center, explain to the tutor that this is a practice exercise and that you would like help with the specific area you focused on.
4. Use your editing log to record any repeated mistakes you've made so that you can be aware of them and try to eliminate them in future writing assignments. (See H2-g for advice about editing logs.)

Directions for extensive practice (focus on fluency and speed)

1. Choose one of the prompts beginning on page H-47 and set aside a specific amount of time to write (fifteen minutes, thirty minutes, or one

hour, for example). Pay special attention to the suggested writing focus in the prompt (or any other focus your instructor recommends).
2. Begin writing and try not to stop until the end of the period you have set. You might find it helpful to set an alarm or a timer.
3. When you are finished, reread your work and highlight the parts of your writing that you like best.
4. If you feel comfortable, read your work to someone else—a roommate, friend, or spouse.
5. Keep your extensive writing in a folder or binder so that you can refer to it as a source of ideas for future writing assignments.

Writing prompts

1. In a paragraph or an essay, discuss the attributes of a person who has had a significant impact on history. *Suggested writing focus:* verb tenses and forms.
2. Write a paragraph or an essay about a time when you were afraid. What did you do? How did you overcome your fear? *Suggested writing focus:* verb tenses and forms.
3. Spend a few minutes reflecting on the last five years of your life. In a paragraph or an essay, describe how you have changed during this time. *Suggested writing focus:* verb tenses and forms.
4. Imagine that you could give advice to any historical figure. To whom would you give advice? What would that advice be? Write a dialogue (a conversation) in which you give this person the advice you think he or she needs. *Suggested writing focus:* modal verbs (for example, "you could . . . ," "you should . . .").
5. Write a paragraph or an essay that describes your goals in life. Remember to consider not only your educational or career aspirations but your personal and emotional goals as well. *Suggested writing focus:* gerunds and infinitives following verbs (for example, "I would like *to live* . . ." or "I can imagine *working* . . .").
6. Think about some of the English idioms and expressions you know that relate to the concept of time. (*Time is money, Time flies, There's no time like the present, To waste time,* and *To spend time* are just a few.) In a paragraph or an essay, explain what you think these expressions reflect about American culture. (Why, for example, do Americans *not* use the expression *There's no time like the past*?) *Suggested writing focus:* sentence completeness and sentence structure.
7. If you could be invisible for a day, where would you go and what would you do? Write a paragraph or an essay in which you describe your intentions or desires. *Suggested writing focus:* conditional sentences.
8. Visit an art museum or gallery and spend a few minutes looking closely at a piece of art that intrigues you. If that is not convenient, look around your campus for a painting or statue that interests you. Write a paragraph or an essay describing the work of art in detail. *Suggested writing focus:* articles or prepositions.

9. Sit down near a busy place on campus (or any other place you spend much of your time). Take a few minutes to observe the people and things around you. Write a paragraph or an essay describing what you see. *Suggested writing focus:* adjectives and adjective clauses.

10. Skim through the editorials or advice columns of a newspaper or magazine. Choose one that interests you. In a paragraph or a brief essay, write a summary of the article, making sure to include the author's main idea. *Suggested writing focus:* understanding main ideas.

11. In a well-organized essay, discuss the advantages (or disadvantages) of living with a roommate. Include a thesis statement and at least three supporting paragraphs. *Suggested writing focus:* thesis and support.

12. In a well-organized essay, discuss the *negative* impacts of a particular invention that is usually considered positive (such as the cell phone, the computer, or the microwave oven). *Suggested writing focus:* paragraph development.

13. In a well-organized essay, compare your personality to the personality of a close friend. (Who is more introverted, for example? Who takes more risks?) *Suggested writing focus:* using transitions between ideas.

14. Think about a social problem that bothers you or a social issue that you feel strongly about. In a well-organized essay, discuss the problem or issue and explain what should be done to improve the situation. Use information from two or three sources. Document your sources with in-text citations and include a works cited page. *Suggested writing focus:* citing sources in MLA style (see MLA-4 in *A Writer's Reference*).

15. Most colleges in the United States value creative thinking over memorization (see H1-b). In a well-organized essay, compare the negative aspects and positive aspects of these two ways of learning and then explain which one you think is preferable. Ask two friends or classmates what they think. Use their responses and your own reasons as evidence to support your position. Be sure to integrate the words or ideas of others into your essay. *Suggested writing focus:* integrating sources (see MLA-3 in *A Writer's Reference*).

Answers to exercises

Exercise H1–1, page H-37

1. When she got home, Mina realized that she had forgotten to buy staples while she was out.
2. Martin Luther King Jr., the famous orator and civil rights activist, delivered his famous "I Have a Dream" speech on August 28, 1963.
3. David has played [or has been playing] soccer for the last fifteen years.
4. Mangoes, which originally grew only in Asia, now grow in the Eastern and Western Hemispheres.
5. Correct
6. Alexander Fleming discovered penicillin while he was working at a hospital in London.
7. Moving to a new country often causes people to change their lifestyles.
8. Although anthropologists do not know exactly when the first calendar was invented, they have evidence that solar calendars have existed for at least six thousand years.
9. When they moved here, my husband and his brother opened a small restaurant.
10. Professors in the United States often require their students to work in groups.

Exercise H1–2, page H-38

1. Woody Guthrie was one of the best-known American folk singer–activists.
2. Born in 1912, Guthrie spent his early life surrounded by music in his small hometown of Okema, Oklahoma.
3. Before his twentieth birthday, he moved to Texas, where he attempted to start a career as a musician.
4. Correct
5. Guthrie and his family moved west to California along with many other Texans and Oklahomans who found employment as farmworkers.
6. While he was traveling, he was exposed to the harsh treatment the migrant workers received.
7. By the time Guthrie arrived in California, he had developed a deep sense of resentment for the rich owners who exploited poor farmworkers.
8. He began writing and singing more songs about workers' rights and political protest, including his most famous song, "This Land Is Your Land."
9. He continued writing songs with a political edge for the rest of his life and motivated many other popular folk and rock singers to carry on his legacy.
10. Today, Guthrie's music lives on in younger generations of people who feel inspired by his words.

Exercise H1–3, page H-38

    Since I was only eight years old, I have dreamed of becoming a professional baseball player. Trying to develop the skill of a professional player has been both physically and mentally challenging. One of the greatest difficulties that I have faced is fear. When I became the pitcher on my high school team, I was under a lot of pressure; my teammates, coach, and all the students at my school depended on me to win games. The thought of losing terrified me. Before a few games in my first season, I put so much pressure on myself to win and to be a good leader that I froze. In time, though, I learned to manage my stress and to make the fear work in my favor. By the time I was a senior, I had transformed the fear into energy that helped me stay alert and quick. Although I know I will have many more challenges to face in pursuit of my dream, I am confident that some day I will succeed.

Exercise H1–4, page H-39

Haley: Good morning, Professor Weil. May I ask you for some advice about my course work?

Professor Weil: Sure, Haley. What can I help you with?

H: I would like to change my major. I'm enrolled as a biology major now, but I am not as interested in science as I thought I would be.

P: I see. What major are you thinking of?

H: Since I am very good at math, I think I would like to be a business major.

P: That's a good idea, but can you do well in classes that don't involve math?

H: I think so. Which courses must I take besides math?

P: You will have to take some communications and writing courses.

H: I can do that. I will go to the registrar and select my courses. Thank you, Professor Weil!

Exercise H1–5, page H-39

Most people think of a trash bin as a finishing point rather than a starting point. However, a recycling bin can be the start of a new life for a piece of paper. After paper is put into an office bin, it is shipped to a recycling center, where it is sorted into types: office paper, cardboard, or colored paper. After it is sorted, it is sent to a paper mill, where it is chopped into dry pulp. The pulp is then mixed with water to form a wet substance called "slurry." The slurry is sent through a screen, which removes little bits of excess materials such as glue, plastic, or staples. After it goes through the screen, the slurry is rinsed again to remove inks. Then the slurry goes through a machine that makes the paper fibers grow bigger. Next the slurry is watered down and placed on a screen, where it is pressed into long, thin sheets and dried on heated rollers. The dried sheets are rolled up and shipped off to other companies where they are processed and made into the paper products we use every day.

Exercise H1–6, page H-40

1. If the governor is reelected, she will not raise the income tax.
2. I could not park my car next to the library because all of the spaces were taken.
3. Sadly, a cure for AIDS has not been found yet.
4. The book that we have to buy for our ecology class is not very expensive.
5. I tried to make a photocopy, but the copier was not functioning properly.
6. Sunnie did not come with us to the football game last Saturday.
7. Although Omar does not like to drive in traffic, he likes to race cars on the weekends.
8. Snow leopards are not extinct, but they are on the endangered species list.
9. Kim could not find lychees [or any lychees] at the supermarket because they are not very common in the United States.
10. I was disappointed that I didn't know the woman's name.

Exercise H1–7, page H-40

1. If Deborah had arrived earlier, she might have found a better parking space.
2. I'll buy you a soda if you come to the cafeteria with me.
3. Correct
4. Correct
5. If I were a famous actor, I would move to Bel Aire and buy a mansion.
6. If you use aloe on a burn, you can reduce the chances of developing a scar.
7. You will have to pay late charges if you don't return your rental video on time.
8. Unless the Security Council agrees, the UN will not send peacekeeping troops to war-torn countries.
9. When Rosa left for college every September, she closed her summer gardening business. *Or* When Rosa leaves for college every September, she closes her summer gardening business.
10. If Kevin were here with us today, he would be enjoying himself.

Exercise H1–8, page H-41

When I was young, my family and I went on an annual camping trip in the canyons of the southwestern United States. One summer, I convinced my family to take a tour of several canyons: the Grand Canyon, Bryce Canyon, and Canyonlands National Park. I remember being amazed at each stop along the way. I loved looking up at the twisting towers of red rock, wondering how they had avoided falling down in the last several thousand years. (I can recall thinking that some might fall over if someone in the canyon sneezed a little too hard.) Even at that young age, I sensed the power of these remarkable landmarks and understood the spell that they had held over so many generations of residents and visitors. In my heart, I promised to go back to the canyons every year. Though I never planned to give up my promise, the commitments of adulthood have prevented me from taking annual trips back to the canyons. I miss visiting the red rocks on a regular basis, but I still manage to go back to the Southwest every few years. Breathing in the high desert air while gazing up at the red rock towers never ceases to refresh and rejuvenate me.

Exercise H2–1, page H-41

When I was only a boy, I was known for being lazy. Every time my parents asked me to clean my room or study for my classes, I always found an excuse to avoid the work. Sometimes I would pretend that I was too tired; other times I would pretend that I had simply forgotten their request. Most of the time, however, I would try to approach the situation logically, arguing that since my older brother was stronger and had more life experience, he should be responsible for most of the household chores.

However, when I started college, my life changed. I realized that in order to become the successful college student I wanted to be, I would have to take control of my life, change my bad habits, and act responsibly. Now I am no longer the lazy boy my parents knew when I was a child. I wake up early, exercise, and go to school. I am never late to my classes, and I always turn my assignments in on time. Although I am still far from perfect, I try to help others whenever I can. Whenever someone needs me, particularly at school or at home, I never try to hide as I did when I was just a boy.

Exercise H2–2, page H-42

It is common to think that being the oldest child in a family has the most privileges. However, there are several advantages to being the youngest child, too. First, it is important to note that by the time the youngest child is born, the parents have already had experience as parents. They know how to care for a newborn, and they tend to be more relaxed. Second, the youngest child has the opportunity to learn how to stay out of trouble. If the older children get into trouble, it is easy for the youngest child to learn from the older children's mistakes. A third advantage of being the youngest child is that in many cases, the youngest gets extra attention from the older siblings. It is not unusual to see older siblings taking care of their younger siblings at school or protecting them from bullies.

Exercise H2–3, page H-42

Possible revisions:

1. Coming to the United States changed more than my address. It changed the direction of my career.
2. My life here in Gainesville is different from the life that I lived in Bolivia.
3. Correct
4. I attended a culinary school, which was the best in Bolivia, and I was offered the chance to study for a short time in the United States.
5. When I first came, I met other students who had different majors.
6. Correct
7. Jin helped me realize the importance of having business experience.
8. I learned that although I enjoyed being a chef, I didn't want to be a chef without business knowledge.
9. I decided to stay a bit longer in the United States, where I could study international business.
10. Someday I will combine both interests and start my own chain of specialized restaurants, which I hope to build all over the world.

Exercise H2–4, page H-43

1. I have never seen a player hit a baseball so hard.
2. Sue cooked the soup very slowly so that the vegetables would be tender.
3. Correct
4. After I finished my workout, I carefully stretched my tender muscles.
5. The professor seemed surprised that the class finished the exam so quickly.
6. After I read the user manual, I easily installed the new hard drive.
7. My mother always told me that she loved all her children equally.
8. As soon as I got the keys to my new car, I drove my friends everywhere.
9. The government found out that the company manufactured the drug illegally.
10. Although she had a difficult time in the past, this year she very easily won the gold medal in cross-country skiing.

Exercise H3–1, page H-43

1. When people move to a new place, they definitely have to go through some changes.
2. The temperature dropped twenty degrees in a half hour yesterday.
3. Some governments help couples who have more than two children by giving them health insurance.
4. When people are too busy, they sometimes forget to eat dinner.

5. Students are exposed to new experiences when they move to a new country.
6. I chose to have a small family so that I could give my children sufficient attention.
7. Marco became more familiar with nature when he studied in the rain forests of Brazil.
8. Let me give you some advice: Buy your books early.
9. A common effect of culture shock is loneliness.
10. Because our school doesn't allow cars within the campus gates, I walk from my parking spot to the place where I need to go.

Exercise H3–2, page H-44

Heifer International is a nonprofit organization that provides animals to poor farmers and families around the world. The organization was started in the 1940s by a man named Dan West, a relief worker who gave people food during times of crisis. West realized that he could help people even more by giving them animals that could supply food — such as milk and cheese — for several years. He wanted to help people for the long term, and he wanted to help them have pride in themselves. Now Heifer serves communities in more than one hundred countries around the world. Its mission is to help families by providing some animals that the families can use to support themselves or start small businesses.

Exercise H3–3, page H-44

Possible revisions:

A greeting is the way that a person addresses or acknowledges another person when the two meet. Types of greetings vary in different countries. People in Japan often prefer to greet nonverbally, with a bow and a smile. An African would likely greet a fellow African with a handshake. For the Maori people of New Zealand, the most common greeting is the *hongi*, which involves rubbing noses. In Poland, a kiss on each cheek is customary; but the Dutch custom is to kiss the right cheek, then the left, and then the right again. A traveler to another country would be wise to learn the greetings expected by its people.

Exercise H4–1, page H-44

1. confusing
2. tiring
3. boring
4. working
5. fascinating
6. handwritten, typed
7. satisfied
8. hand-painted
9. cleaning
10. peeled

Exercise H5–1, page H-45

1. Does your dance class start on Monday or Wednesday?
2. Correct

3. As soon as Fiona moved into her dorm room, she put a poster of Einstein on the wall for inspiration.
4. My books are a little dusty because they were packed away in the garage for a year.
5. Dr. Horn is taking his students to Ghana for a study trip in early June.
6. My grandmother was born in Los Angeles, but my grandfather was born in Albuquerque.
7. My fraternity brothers like to play loud music on the street in front of our building.
8. My exam begins in two hours, but I'm not nervous at all.
9. Correct
10. Bret finished writing his term paper right at midnight.

Exercise H5–2, page H-45

1. I have trouble concentrating on my homework when my roommate is around.
2. The senator was skilled at delaying controversial votes.
3. I'm not worried about our verbs test on Wednesday.
4. While Ellie proofread the group's report, Sam and Tomi worked on the presentation slides.
5. Correct
6. The solution consists of sodium and water.
7. I was afraid to board the plane because I'm not accustomed to traveling alone.
8. Shea remained devoted to the teachings of his martial arts master.
9. You can always count on Carole to help out when the office gets busy.
10. Correct

Index